Spiral Bound

Table of Contents

Alice Drowning

Alice Drowning

At first they thought she was pregnant. Then somebody spent an afternoon online and decided the problem was probably in her inner ears—in those little semicircular canals that house the human sense of balance. Or perhaps it was plain vertigo? Chronic nausea? Is that a thing, *chronic nausea?*

The neighbors called with a dozen suggested remedies. But nothing helped or hurt her. She stumbled through her daily chores for years, catching herself on countertops and chairbacks, before receiving a proper diagnosis.

It turned out that Alice—who had never left Nebraska—was terminally seasick.

Irrespective of her circumstances, Alice was destined to drown at sea. And whether her end roared up from platinum waves with a trident in his fist, or simply held her round white cheek to the linoleum—that was her fated end.

For her part, Alice had known it from the start. If her careworn mother had thought to review the crayon drawings of twenty years before, she'd have found a girl (indicated with yellow spiral curls) at home with giant fish (drawn with one continuous line, like a figure eight on its side with one edge blunted). She suffered nightmares with no pictures—just the sound of her heart beating hard and fast. Then hard and very slow. She stargazed obsessively, gripped by an unromantic impulse to memorize the constellations as they swept across the black expanse of prairie sky. In high school, the hardest years, she salted her bath water. But by her early twenties, she was nearly oblivious to the constant motion. She rebounded from dishwasher to dinner table, accustomed to the whirl and tilt. Protracted melancholy is a hazard at sea, and self-pity is unbecoming conduct of a sailor.

When they found her, calm and blue, her lungs were full of brine.

The Greatest Remove

The Greatest Remove

To extricate yourself from your daily chores and errands, you are most thoroughly removed by a gram and a half of opium from Manali. It comes wrapped in printed foil, disguised as a silver bead. In this way it is overlooked by the men at the airport who are searching for it in the heels of shoes, or in hollow bracelets, or in the false bottoms of real suitcases, or however else it came in last year.

Manali is the most remote you can get. The walls of your brain go smooth and the ghosts of your concerns sweep past, unable to gain purchase.

Legally, the furthest you can go is to another person. A new, sexually attractive person. By the love scene, when the story's all but over, you may find your numberless anxieties returning to you. But in the hour before any definite commitment has been forged, your brain is wholly occupied by the intrigue. You are racing the clock above the bar to create an impression that can land all the little dials set to yes. You are walking in a piano, stepping string to string: you must pass over all the tripwire, must sound only those notes that beautify the conversation, that make you funny and smart and not too practiced in the process. Here your brain is too full of static charge and rum to pay any notice to the buzz of apprehension that vibrates your adulthood like a never-ending passing train.

Of course this method, in the morning, often contributes one more voice to those that must be muted to achieve another quiet moment.

The greatest distance that can by obtained by legal, modest means is provided by an American-style carwash.

It's very hard to feel safe in safe places. In pastoral settings, or in the arms of your great love, a considerable stake is implied. Serene moments, by their nature, are the most vulnerable to disruption. A carwash addresses these mammalian fears directly. A carwash says: Yes, there is danger all about. You are in the epicenter of an oceanic hell, the heart of a great turquoise volcano— the worst has come to pass. And yet somehow you are surviving. All the strength of man and God is battering the glass, and you are dry and warm in a diving bell. With a stereo.

Sometimes the bell advances of its own accord, sometimes a light emerges from the hurricane to prompt you to pull forward. Inch by inch, you return to the world, which has been dissolved and rebuilt with all the soot and trash since you went under.

Sleeping on the Stairs

It is 4:23 in the morning. I am at the top of the beautiful, stupid staircase in my head.

Three months ago, during a trip to the dentist, I realized that I needed a staircase.

I arrived late to the appointment, struggling to contain the contents of an overburdened manila file. I opened the door with my hip while my right hand operated independently to check all my pockets in a futile search for my cell phone. The receptionist kindly accepted my little bow of apology and waved me in.

I go to a low-income clinic for artists where I seldom see the same dentist. This means that the novocaine talk must be had anew on every visit.

I looked into to a pair of large, brown eyes above a paper mask. "I have a pretty incredible tolerance to novocaine." (This presentation is infinitely preferable to the converse formulation: I have a terrible sensitivity to pain.)

"Well, I'll keep that in mind."

I didn't believe this new dentist *would* keep that in mind. I believed that she had forgotten it already. I'm a relatively slender young woman and so dentists are reluctant to dose me as I'd like to be dosed. Which is as an elk calf.

The dentist began to prepare what I guessed to be a

grossly inadequate shot of novocaine. Partially reclined in her padded chair, I regarded a magazine page taped to the ceiling. It featured a sandy sweep of ocean, a tropical dental getaway. I do not like to pretend I am in Mexico when I am receiving medical attention, even just for fun. The dentist administered my shot; the hygienist attended to her shining instruments; and we waited for my face to go numb.

Sensing the opportunity, my mind immediately shot off. It flipped through the remembered contents of my calendar, called out approaching deadlines, then scrawled a harried to-do list whose items ticked past too quickly to read. My mind, which I used to consider a great ally, has turned into a sparrow on a leash. A crazy-ambitious, unblinking sparrow, amped up on cocaine with red kaleidoscope eyes. It keeps me up at night. It talks over my phone calls. It strains toward the next task even before I'm finished eating, before I'm out of the shower, before I've properly greeted people, or put the car in park. More troubling, it seems to *like me* less and less.

The dentist revved her drill, "Alright, let's give it a try."

After thirty seconds of cautious drilling, I flinched beneath her.

"You're feeling me?"

"Uh-huh."

"Something cold or something sharp?"

I moved my hands.

"You're not sure. Okay, hang in there."

She refilled her syringe and talked me through a series of injections, "Now I'm going to walk it backwards a bit here, good, breathe for me."

In the midst of the fourth shot, I wondered how much farther she'd have to sink the needle to get the sparrow. After a few sore minutes of waiting, we were able to continue, this time quite confidently. The dentist dispensed with her former delicacy and chatted with the hygienist as if they were alone in the room.

The drill sent up little clouds of toothdust. I felt the numbness advance unevenly across my face—the way that armies advance across a map of Europe. The numb took over the left side of my nose, but could not bridge the septum. I felt it overtake the outer edge of my left eye, as though I was blinking someone else's lid. It occurred to me that I had asked for too much novocaine. That perhaps I was getting brain damage. But I couldn't drum up much concern. I was painless; I wasn't late for anything; and the vibration in my jaw suppressed any real rumination. Quite possibly in the midst of a chemical lobotomy, my only definite thought was: *It feels so good to lie down.*

That's when I knew that I needed a staircase. A filling appointment is not supposed to be the most tranquil part of the day. I resolved that as soon as I left the chair, I'd start studying meditation, or mindful living, or eating flax seeds—whatever it took to dial down.

I'd resisted the staircase method in the past, because it seemed so New Agey. People who put themselves to sleep by envisioning their descent down a mental staircase are people who confer great agency to crystals. They are people who read books about spiritual healing with covers that feature pastel drawings of buxom fairies in prayer.

Yet here I am, in the early hours of the morning, atop my very own flight of brainstairs.

Self-hypnosis is sort of like trying to perform a card trick on yourself. The talking part of your brain must convince the rest of your brain to go to sleep without seeming too calculated. It has to seem casual. The details of the process vary, but my narrative goes like this:

You are standing at the top of a beautiful, white staircase in the middle of a golden pond.

You will descend this staircase, into the iridescent water. With every step you'll become more relaxed; the tension will lift out of your body and dissipate on the surface of the pond.

Let's begin...

So it goes, very deliberate and controlled, as I effectively drown myself to sleep. Although it's nearly foolproof now, it didn't work right away. At the beginning when I felt myself drifting into sleep, the thrill of success would snap me back into full consciousness. Or I'd get impatient and take the steps too fast. When the water was at my shoulders a little voice of panic spoke over the hypnotist, *This is not working*, NOT WORKING.

Before my staircase, sleep seemed binary: I was doing it or I was not. I've now become familiar with the gradations of consciousness. On the first step I am impatient, hyperaware of every itch, unhappy to be on a staircase. On the second step I am better able to actually focus on the parts of my body that are asked to release. Between steps three and four, I find that my mind has taken an unauthorized vacation—just a little sweep of nonsense, maybe in the flash of a remembered conversation or a brief visit from some imagined third party. This recognition is usually enough to fully reinstall me on the staircase. I continue. But then, with the water at my waist, I find I have lifted my foot but can't remember where to put it. Or I find that I have been standing still for what seems like a very long time. At that point I have only a few remaining moments of lucidity.

In truth, I do not know what happens after that. Presumably my limp body tumbles down, in the slow motion of an underwater fall. I lie at the foot of the stairs for hours. The current lifts my hair. Far away, other climbers roll down their own staircases and hit the bottom in a little plume of soft dust. I remain crumpled, breathing slowly until a pair of divers arrives to lift me to the surface where another day is breaking. Perched on the dry landing above, my sparrow looks on, waiting.

A Little Note
on All of It

A Little Note on All of It

Life,
life is bad.
But people are good.
Regrettably, life is the only way to animate people.
They are otherwise slack dolls
slumped over their desks
whose limbs must be
stuffed through the holes in their clothing.

Life is a clumsy instrument,
the heavy key to wind a spring.
Life is also, incidentally,
the only good distraction
from my impending death.

My New Purpose

Without me,
how would my headache
get around?

Saint Maxwell

Saint Maxwell

When my little brother Max was born, the priest refused to baptize him. Tapping the Jerusalem Bible, he told my parents, "You must select another name, there is no Saint Maxwell." My dad, with his only son in his arms and his only tie around his neck, responded, "If we don't name any boys Max, how are we going to get one?"

The summer of 1989, Max turned the same color head to toe. He was four years old. The sun bleached his hair to match his tan exactly. My dad nicknamed him Coppertop and I set a new penny on his tiny upturned nose to admire the camouflage effect.

Two years later, Max fell victim to his first bee sting. Limp-skipping, he ran into my open arms and buried his face in my stomach. He could not be consoled. Thinking the kid might be going anaphylactic, I asked, "Maxie does it really hurt so badly?" No, he shook his head. In the diaphragm spasms of the after-cry he stammered, "I, I, I just don't know why he did it." Maxie knew already that an enemy was worse than any wound.

Sometimes Max and I accompanied our father to the airfield. My father taught other pilots how to fly gliders, light one-man planes that are barely more than varnished kites. Driving down the grass runways, my dad taught me the nomenclature of clouds; he'd point out a specimen and I'd say *cumulonimbus* or *nimbostratus*. One afternoon, he threw the question back to Max, curled up on the backseat. "Maxwell," my father slowed the car to center a cumulus in the windshield, "Name that cloud." Maxie clambered to his knees to peer over the bench seat. He blinked once then announced, "Alex Rasmussen."

"Excellent work!" My father drummed the dashboard, driving with his knees. "Alex Rasmussen. What a great name for a cloud."

At sixteen, Max suffered his first thorough heartbreak. Speaking of the sensation and the long recovery that followed, he remarked, "I've come to the conclusion that if you hit rock bottom hard enough… you will bounce."

When Max was seventeen, I was diagnosed with an ovarian tumor. After many ultrasounds and great expense, the specialist announced that the tumor was mobile and that it had to come out. I imagined my tumor in a tiny biplane, with a little leather helmet, motoring around and around my right ovary.

Max came to the hospital with me. From check-in to the time I was wheeled into the operating room, I don't remember him blinking. He held my hand and flirted with the nurses. Looking up at him smiling down, I fought the anesthesia to the black end.

During the operation, I floated through memories and sedation-dreams.

On a road trip as a kid, I woke up in the middle of the night while my father drove through Gary, Indiana.

The slender spires of the industrial plants rose up studded with white lights. Whirling steam glowed in the high beams. Drowsy in the backseat, I asked if we had made it to the Emerald City.

The surgery was a success. Now it's just a pretty good scar. But Max and I have noticed the change.

Both of us are now young adults who can curse in each other's company, and drink, and stay up all night. We will speak at each other's weddings; we will help to raise each other's kids; one day we will bury my father and his tie. And ultimately, one of us will speak at the other's funeral.

People die—yes, yes we know that. But Max and I have come to really appreciate that some people die *first*. I'm older. But then girls live longer. Anyone's guess really.

Yesterday at 8 a.m., Maxie arrived in Barcelona. He wrote me an email that agreed: Yes, the Spanish girls are prettier than the French. For him it is the summer before college. He graduated high school by an uncomfortably narrow margin; he can grow a ridiculous beard; and he is backpacking Europe, following a route I took years ago. At the end of his email, he asked, "Any suggestions for your little bro?"

I have not yet written him back. But if I can explain it right, I will say: Maxwell trust your intuition, and select your landmarks very carefully. Much of what you see now may erode before you return. And know that when you need me—even half a world away—if I'm breathing, I'll come get you. When you finally call for me and I don't answer, go to Gary. I'll meet you there. They hid paradise in the last place anyone would look.

The Jacket Dove

The Jacket Dove

The scarves whisk down his shirtsleeves
and I know we're near the end.

I hear the children's voices,
chirping far away,
their horror and delight
a challenge to discern.

My neck is turned against his pocket
where it smells of starch and sweat,
where his giant heart is beating
half as slow as death.

With my feet pinched between his fingers,
he reveals me to a blinding light.
The world flares up around me—
in a dozen colors I'd forgotten—
before the satin lining snuffs it out.

Here in the heat my kindness fails me.
If he had a wishbone, I would break it,
sing the morning song til dark.

But there is nothing in him
to snap or shake or soften.
He is a hollow-bodied thing
built to hide some silver trinkets,
and a set of useless wings.

Nostalgia

Nostalgia

Nostalgia comes home late,
the lovely tired little drunk,
hair let loose and curling at the ends.
In the darkness of the living room
and in her stocking feet,
she tip toes to the couch
with exaggerated sneaking—
knees lifting almost to her chest
and arms outstretched like airplane wings—
to pass out limp and dreaming in her dress.

She does not see me in the doorway
a shadow leaning heavy on the frame,
the hollows of my eyes gone blue
a dozen years ago.

My vanity and my good looks
had the decency to leave together.
There is some mercy, after all, in our design:
a soft amnesia for the frequently mistreated,
an adrenal surge for the cornered and outnumbered,
a flash of light for the very nearly dead.

Nostalgia

If I could sweep together all my scraps of time:
the leap years in my arms,
and the hours lost in airplanes
flying east against the turning world,
I'd stitch them front to end
and weave a garland
like waterlily crown,
lay it wet and heavy
on Nostaglia's dizzy head of sunbleached hair.

Her even sleeping sounds
bounce lightly off the walls and floor
compounding ad infinitum
in the echo chamber of our home.

She is indifferent company,
a member of the privileged caste
exempt from housework, boredom,
and the stickypaper of intimate association.

Still, I can't resist the waif
flushed pink, and posed
exactly as she fell.

She is timesick,
drunk and lovely.
I am just an incidental:
the kindly aging organism
that puts her down to bed.

The Leviathan

Men who have been told too often that their eyes are beautiful are reluctant to blink them. They're so keenly aware of the asset that it hinders natural conversation. Life was not like this. Either his former lovers were sparing with their praise (for which I would thank them) or he had tamed his vanity—which is unusual in young men. Whatever the case, he did not leverage his blue-green eyes. He blinked them and rubbed them and closed them to kiss. He moved them all around to see where he was going, just as the rest of us would do. But every time they connected with mine for more than a moment, my mind went white, like a needle had been lifted from the record in my head.

I met Life in a standing line. I was in Uruguay, backpacking South America. Both of us were waiting to withdraw cash from a machine in the lobby of a bank. There was a problem with the device; I overheard it described with a word I did not know. A technician arrived and swung open the faceplate of the ATM to reveal the insect machinery within—matted wires, biting gears, and mean little moving parts. News passed down the line, sometimes translated lazily into French, that the device would not function for another twenty minutes. I received notice from the girl in front of me and turned to pass it back. And there was Life, in a fashionable jacket with an aviator's collar, grinning at me.

Hobbes had it precisely backwards with his *poor, nasty, brutish, and short.* Life is tall, benevolent, and perilously slender with harpoon-blue eyes. He had a five o'clock shadow, flashing white teeth, and a bouncing swagger—like James Dean walking on the moon.

His name was spelled Leif, which was misleading because it provoked the mispronunciation Leaf. Every time he introduced himself, he had to coach new acquaintances to say his name correctly. Then, unfailingly, he nursed them through their disbelief.

"Not Life like…life?"

"Yes."

"*Life?* Like life and death?"

"Yes, just like that."

"Hey," The face of the speaker would illuminate with a growing sense of his own cleverness. "Life is short! Ha! Life is cheap! Ha!" My new friend Life would wait patiently until the idioms were spent and the introductions could continue.

I made the same sorry jokes at our first meeting in front of the ATM. I reddened later when I realized how often he suffered them. In the three days I spent with Life, I heard the same tiresome exchange two dozen times.

Definite routes emerge among backpackers. Almost everyone is going where you are headed, or they are going to the place you have most recently been. We go like forest ants, wearing light footpaths into the surface of the planet and carrying loads disproportionate to our small bodies. We tend to read the same books, something topical to the world passing through the bus windows. In South America, everyone is reading *The Motorcycle Diaries*. Most people are trying to get a hold of *The Alchemist*. Everybody coming from Asia has just finished *Life of Pi*. The impromptu travelers' libraries that emerge on backpacker routes have a few titles, but they appear in dozens of translations.

Life and I were both en route to Montevideo, the capital city. We exchanged abridged biographies in the accelerated fashion of travelers. Life was German. Twenty-seven. A paramedic. (*Is that the word?* Yes, that is the word. *My English is too bad.* No, your English is very good.) He had just finished a two-year term as a critical care nurse in a Bolivian hospital. I was an American on holiday. Twenty-five. A rapper. (*A rapper!* Yes, a rapper. *How unusual your job!* How unusual your name. *Ah, this is true; we are being unusual together.*)

We caught the evening train, drinking grappa and peach juice from a can to hide it from the conductor. Late that night, in a rented hostel bed, and without a lot of ceremony, we had sex. Life was pale and lovely but desperately—dangerously—thin. An anatomical sketch on bleached paper. I was full-lipped and slender, pretty enough, but with a grey-eyed look of perpetual exhaustion. I admit there's an edge to my disposition that's visible even at a glance. My impatience makes it hard to sleep and I'm prone to a melancholy that hollows out my cheeks. But our room was dim; in it Life glowed like a moon, and I'm sure none of my severity was evident in silhouette. We were a fine, brief pair.

In the morning Life and I wandered through Montevideo. The streets were wide and grey and completely empty. "Who lives in this city?" We asked each other at a silent café. "Where are they now?"

We drifted by the few vendors on the sidewalk, and I paused to examine the wares of a bedraggled looking young couple. They sat cross-legged on a floor rug laid out on the pavement. I stooped to pick up a glass bottle from their rug. It was filled with a light yellow liquid. "What is it?"

The female member of the pair answered with a long phrase I didn't know. I looked up at Life, who shrugged.

"It's alcohol," the woman said. "A native drink to here." She pointed down to the rug, presumably indicating Uruguay more generally.

"Is it sweet?" I asked the vendor.

"Yes," the man answered, "it is made from eggs."

Life kicked me lightly and made a very strained face, trying to mentally communicate all the potential hazards of drinking such a product purchased on the street. I'm hopeless when it comes to sugary boozy things, and so I bought it over his telepathic objection.

Out of earshot he warned me, "You will die if you drink this."

"Probably. I'll trust you to revive me."

We rounded a corner and arrived in a central square, where I found the only real attraction Montevideo held for me. An iron soldier, several stories high, sat on horseback. He was badly weathered; years of pooling rain had blackened his eye sockets and stained his cheeks in little rivulets. The effect was Oedipal. With no apparent opponent, the looming soldier seemed equally magnificent and ridiculous: a leviathan standing guard over an empty city, blinded by rain.

Life asked me, "Do you know how to read the legs?" He explained that horses are deliberately positioned in war memorials to indicate the fate of the rider. If all four feet are on the ground, the rider survived unharmed. If one hoof is lifted, the rider was wounded in battle. If the horse rears on its hind legs, the rider was killed.

My rider had been maimed.

We stood quietly for a while, then Life put his hand on the small of my back. "Your shoe is open." He pointed to the untied laces of my right tennis shoe. I knelt to tie a bow, then took his hand to resume our walk.

Back at the hostel, we sat on the edge of Life's bed. He showed me the contents of his pack: gauze and pills with Spanish labels. He pulled out little glass bottles full of liquid morphine. They had no caps, they just tapered in the middle where the nurse was expected to snap them open. I had seen others like them in old war movies.

"Do you ever cut yourself?"

He nodded. "Always. At the beginning only sometimes I didn't cut myself."

I expected he would bring those bottles back to Germany to show his nursing friends at home how archaic were the means of his South American station. Some of the bottles, I thought, he will use recreationally.

We went downstairs to a communal kitchen and dining room. I opened my little bottle liquor from the street, Life made a face, and forbade me from entering the kitchen while he cooked. I joined a long table filling for the dinner hour.

Hostel talk is some of the frankest conversation in the world. In an itinerant community, all homesick and hungry for connection, there's very little call for restraint. Anything you say or do will be erased from public memory by next week. It must be something like marriage to an amnesiac. If you are so inclined, you can say things like 'Let's have sex' or 'Your arrogance repels me' after fifteen minutes of acquaintance. And this tenor is the same around the world—conversations from a hundred wooden tables blur into a continuous story reel of love and horror, drunken oaths, sex, faith, and revelation. There are people who found God and lost their passports; people who cast aside their caution, drank the water and got the bad disease; people who are not sure they're ever going home; people who talk with one eye on the door, hoping that their plans to rendezvous will be honored by some second party halfway around the world.

Around the table maps drawn are on napkins, and then pressed between the pages of a paperback. Warnings circulate like a contagion: the counterfeiters have found a way to watermark the bills; the taxis with the yellow emblems on the doors are certified, the gypsy cabs will circle the whole forsaken city; the dentists here are lousy, wait til Buenos Aires if you can; Sao Pablo isn't as bad as everyone says; Caracas is worse, arrive in the daylight and when you get there ask for Sandra.

Tank tops expose star-shaped scars on the upper arms of some travelers. It's the mark left by a smallpox vaccination. You can tell who comes from poor countries by these scars—countries where long-conquered diseases still kill people. Even if your family is wealthy enough to send you abroad, the scar shining beneath the straps of your Northface reveals the turmoil of your native place—like all the poverty you left behind kissed you on the shoulder to brand you a deserter.

In Montevideo, every backpacker at the table who had stayed at a particular hostel in Rio had been robbed, one with a ballpoint pen.

The Irish kid kept a Belgian Euro on hand for the important circumstances often determined by a coin toss. The metalwork is considerably heavier on one side; it lands tails more than five times of ten. As a result, he'd enjoyed top bunks and window seats for the better part of a year.

A fellow American testifies that fresh-water dolphins swim in the Bolivian rivers. They are curious about humans and are Easter-egg pink. Three other travelers confirm her description.

A British man named Jack, who was too well aware of his handsomeness, rolled a joint in a hollowed cigarette. He lit it, blew a lousy smoke ring, and then returned to his conversation about piranhas. A girl in cloth bracelets was rapt. The part in her straight blonde hair was marred by a scar where she been hit with the hilt of a machete during a hijacking in Equador. She exhaled from the side of her mouth and nodded to encourage Jack to continue. "…They are blind to meat that isn't bleeding, you see. You can swim with them, unless you are menstruating." We learned that Jack fished for them in the Brazilian Pantenal using a hook baited with chum. After he had pulled one aboard, his friends encouraged him to slip a machete blade into its open mouth. It clamped down ferociously. When the boys removed the blade, they found teeth marks in the tempered steel.

I leaned in to recount a story from my travels India. I'd seen a girl so drugged that the locals said she could not remember her own name. She was Italian, but had lost the passport to prove it. She had waist-length hair and wore Indian clothing. I meant to tell about her encounter with the saddhus that lived beneath the ghats, but my anecdote was interrupted by a pair of new arrivals.

A young couple settled at the table. They had recently come in from Africa and both had white wrinkles at the corners of their eyes. The rotation of the joint was laboriously rerouted to include them and all were eager to engage them in the conversation. They smiled, but stayed quiet while the talk rolled on about thieves and bargains, good drugs and beaches that the book writers hadn't spoiled yet.

In the social order of ex-patriots, this pair was easy royalty. Their tans were darker. They did not rush to boast of their adventures. They leaned against each other and laughed easily at other people's stories. There is a hierarchy to be found wherever more than two people convene; in hostels this order is determined by the length of your stay, your command of the local language, and how modest your means. I remember hoping the new ascetics would favor me.

He pet her wavy hair, and held in a lungful of smoke. When pressed to provide some detail of their recent travels, the female member of the pair offered that in Kenya, the people put unlit cigarettes into the gasoline. *Why?* She was not sure, but the practice was universally observed. *Don't the cigarettes get caught in the engine?* No, no, the tobacco is shaken directly into the gas tank. Cars need one cigarette, trucks get two.

Someone at the other end of the table asked a question that was passed around: "What is your greatest, single fear?" There was a rush of chatter to formulate responses. When it was my turn to answer, I offered, "Death—the process, not the condition." The Irish boy answered, "Irrelevance."

Life emerged from the kitchen, where he had somehow procured a crisp white apron, to tell me that our meals were ready. We sat side by side to eat our chicken and pasta. We then retreated to the balcony of our shared room where the voices of communion grew indistinct. Life lit a cigarette and I asked him to tell me about his work Bolivia. He unearthed a few snapshots.

"What is this?"

"A fuse table. With empanadas on it."

"Why?"

"I don't know, they are for sale in the mornings this way."

"This is you at work?"

"Yes, and in the mask, that is a very good doctor."

"How many patients did you see every day?"

"Well, it depends." He pulled at me gently, so that I rested my head in his lap. "Around Christmas or Carnival, no one came in, for anything. Everybody needed to save their money. Then, like a month later, they would all come. Maybe the man had broken his leg or maybe he had a heart attack the month before and we asked, 'Why are you coming here now, why are you waiting so long?' It was because he needed the money to have a party. For Christmas."

I folded my hands beneath my cheek. "Have you ever fallen in love with a patient?"

"Never." Life reminded me that he was an intensive care nurse.

"Right. I suppose the patients are not really in a position to get involved."

"Correct." Life's smile was slow and asymmetrical. Only one side of his upper lip lifted, exposing canine teeth. It was an expression tempered by seriousness: a small pull on a weighted line. His whole face never got involved; something impeded the signal and by the time the smile could be telegraphed to all of his features, the happy occasion had passed.

He continued, "For love, it is usually nurse and nurse or doctor and nurse. The patients are not talking, just lying down. The patients are only work."

"Of course."

"The patients are numbers," Life kissed my shoulder. "Numbers with names."

In several pictures Life posed with another young man, both of them looking tousled.

"Who is this?"

"That is Nico, my best friend in Bolivia. Also my roommate."

Life and Nico posed in their in civilian clothes, their long arms slung around each other. Like Life, Nico was handsome, but with darker eyes and hair. Unlike Life, his smile was full—in the photograph it opened his mouth and shut his eyes. As the time stamps on the photographs advanced, their skin darkened, they seemed to shave less frequently, and Life visibly lost weight. It turns out that he was not so thin before his term of service; living at altitude had exacted 30 pounds. Maybe that accounted for his bouncy stride— he was still walking like the heavier man he used to be.

I asked if it was hard to get used to the limited resources of his station in Bolivia. He drew a breath that he did not audibly exhale.

"Very difficult. They had only one heart monitor for three persons." Life detected that I did not fully register the significance of this arrangement. "Also, we used the *jeringa* twice or more times."

"I don't know what that is."

"I knew the English word…Look please," Life pumped his thumb toward the V of his index and middle fingers.

"A syringe—Really? You used them more than once?"

"Yes. And they didn't have gloves. That is crazy. And I thought this is impossible, I am going to get everything. And so at first I test myself all the time for AIDS, for everything. And I became an addict to yellow."

It took us several minutes to resolve this phrase as jaundice, which Life suffered for a portion of his stay.

"What were the most common kinds of cases that you saw?"

"Burns."

"What kind of burns?"

"Water and...*aceite*?"

"Oil. Mostly from the kitchen?"

"Kitchen or from windows. Families, they have like five or eight children. So if they have one more, they are not wanting him. So they try to kill him."

"Jesus. What ages were the children, who they tried to kill?"

"From like one month to ten years."

"Why would they bring them to the hospital then, if they had tried to kill them? Why would they bring them in for help?" I could feel Life's hipbone sharp against my shoulder blade; our skeletons were almost touching.

"Maybe the neighbors called. Or sometimes, it didn't work. So they have him part dead, thinking, 'What do we do with him now?'" Life laughed after he said this. I was not sure why.

"Did it fuck with your head?"

"The first time, yes. The other times...yes. But you have to block it out, if you keep thinking about it, it will make you mad."

I asked Life if he ever felt a connection to a particular case, if he ever felt personally involved. The answer, of course, was Angel Viri.

Life worked his two-year term in La Paz—the highest

capital city in the world. In Spanish the name means *Peace* and like every place-name, the nomenclature has outlasted whatever quality inspired it. In pictures the city is as idiosyncratic as any poor city in Latin America. Grey buildings cascade down a valley, too numerous to be real; lean-to shelters rest against the glass buildings downtown. The view from Life's hospital windows showcased the scale of the metropolis. It was there, in the hospital, that Life met Angel. But by then, Angel was technically already dead.

Angel was a sixteen-year-old street kid. He had a wife and two children. He'd worked with Nico for years through a social program called *Proyecto Calle.* Angel was born with a bad mitral valve, which led to cardiac insufficiency, which meant his heart couldn't pump enough blood. His was the first heart transplant ever attempted at Life's hospital. The facility had been buzzing with Angel's case—it was a landmark operation to attempt. The whole place felt balanced on the threshold of an important, modern change. Although Angel technically survived the transplant, he died ten minutes after the procedure was complete. Life entered the room exactly then—essentially as Angel was leaving—and delayed the doctors who were set to announce the time of death.

"I did this," Life put his hands on top of one another, palms down, and made a little series of timed thrusts.

Life administered CPR for seventy minutes after Angel's new heart stopped beating. I don't know whom the heart belonged to before he got it, and I don't know where Angel's old one went. The doctors allowed Life to continue until his own cramping and exhaustion persuaded him to leave the table. It was a Saturday afternoon. Life left the hospital to find a liquor store, then headed home to find Nico.

By the time Life entered the apartment, Nico had already been notified. The pair installed themselves in front of a window that overlooked the hillside city and drank rum from juice glasses. Life's recollection of the evening fades to black here, through the bottom of an upturned glass.

I didn't think then to ask why a street kid had been the first to receive what must have been an expensive procedure. But it occurs to me now: for practice. And even as a non-believer, the prospect gives me a special chill—who would have the nerve to practice on a kid named Angel? In the hostel, to my discredit, I pressed Life. I asked too many questions, even after I sensed that they dismayed him. The names and places wouldn't let me leave it all alone—I kept coming back for one last pass, looking for something to salvage or decipher. But if there is a larger picture, it is lost on me. And Life. And Nico. Near as I can tell the story has no moral.

In a city called Peace a boy named Angel received a human heart. It failed as soon as it was sewn in place. The boy's short story is some hybrid of youth and horror: part cherub and part seraphim. A nurse called Life could not revive the boy; on failing, he drank himself to dreamless sleep. Peace was as close to heaven as big cities are allowed to get, so it must have been a short trip home for Angel. It will be long for Life who woke up feeling that he was not the servant of a just and greater purpose—that he was not charged to cure or even treat. More often, life is an agent of consolation and all that can be asked, in his fumbling with the morphine, is that that bottle breaks as it's intended.

Camera Obscura

My dad darts and wheels around the tiny cabin of the boat, muttering. Hunting flies.

"Go ahead and fly in circles—fly your little filthy circles. For I am The Hunter. And I do not take prisoners. No I DON'T! Got you. Sorry man, them's the rules when you're on my boat. We don't do appeals. We don't do military burials, no sir. You will be joining your fallen brethren in the garbage pail beneath the sink. Adieu mon frère!"

My father, technically, is a genius. He dismisses the fact, but it's true. When Mensa extended their invitation, he attended one meeting, deemed it populated by snobs, and came home early. He thinks the entire business is a confederacy of the over-privileged. He's a glider pilot now, but over the course of his career he has worked as a concert lute player; a trader on the grain exchange; a technical writer; and an audiologist. Recently, he's gotten into sailing—a feat on the salary of a self-employed glider pilot.

He tosses his hair out of his face and in slow-motion lifts the swatter like a saber, adopting an expression of religious awe. Then, in an accent that is part French and part German: "Evairy-thing I have learned about life und death, I have learned from zee fly. To live… you root en gar-bahge. To die…you are swatted by an unzeen hand."

I believe that my father would have behaved in exactly the same way if he had been alone.

As is, the two of us are spending a brief vacation together aboard his newly acquired sailboat, *The Mary M.* The boat is exceedingly small, with just a single sail. Below deck neither of us can stand quite straight. A couple of crawlspaces serve as sleeping berths. My dad purchased it on the cheap last year, and has spent several months immersed in its renovation. Although he has not admitted to it yet, I firmly believe that my father intends to sail around the world in this boat. In his apartment, piles of sailing books sit on the carpet, edging every room. The last time I visited he was reading a chapter on emergency dentistry, learning how to remove his own teeth with common tools.

After several invitations, I finally took some time away from the city to join my dad aboard the object of his enthusiasm. Unfortunately, my visit brought rough weather. For days, we have eaten and slept aboard *The Mary M*—violently tossed about the cabin as strong waves break against the hull—the whole while tied securely to the marina. Because we anticipate the weather will clear every morning, we do not perceive this to be ridiculous.

I don't know it yet, but I have become very, very landsick. That's the thing about landsickness, you don't know you have it until you get off the boat and the dock lurches beneath you. It's like a drunkenness from which all pleasure has been extracted.

In the evening, my dad and I sit down to dinner. He has prepared steaming plates of curried fish and two stiff Manhattans. I flip a catch on the cabin wall that releases a tiny tabletop, which I lower like a Murphy bed. The quarters are so close that our knees touch beneath the table. Everything on *The Mary M* folds up when you're not using it; seafaring is an origami lifestyle. I have the impression that if I bored him, my father would set my arms at my sides, fold me in two, and stow me in the aft crawlspace.

Every existential crisis begins with an almost imperceptible shift—the thud of a feather. This particular trouble starts at the bottom of my second Manhattan. I am rinsing the dishes, occasionally lifting my drink with a soapy hand, and chatting over my shoulder to my father. He lies on a narrow bench seat with his feet propped against the cabin wall. *He looks like a sailor,* I think. He's thin and tall with dark hair, but his three-day beard has turned mostly white. I've never seen this beard before, it suits him so well it looks artificial, maybe fastening behind his ears. It gives him a Sean Connery look—in *The Hunt for Red October* years. It spooked me when I arrived, however. I had never imagined it would be so grey.

We talk personally only for a moment.

How is Doomtree?

Doomtree is okay.

How is Leslie, his girlfriend?

Leslie is brilliant as ever.

Then we talk art. Music and movies and books and radio shows. Jeff Buckley, the Chaconne in D minor, Ira Glass, and James Thurber.

While pouring another half-glass for each of us, my father recounts an episode from the early days of cinema:

Movies had recently made it to the mainstream, theaters were filling, and a new kind of icon entered cultural consciousness: the film star. Then, abruptly, one of them died. An actor, a star, died while his new film was still in theaters. Audiences were conflicted... was it decent to attend the screening of a dead man? To watch him move around up there, and be entertained by him? The discussion stirred passions and in some places would-be viewers boycotted the film, out of respect for the deceased—or maybe an aversion to the macabre.

This anecdote stuns me for reasons I am still formulating. My dad, oblivious to my reaction, lifts my empty glass out of my hand and slides in the fresh half Manhattan. My hand remains fixed, as though I am a Lego man being armed with a spear. My dad clinks his glass against my immobile one and empties his in two big drafts. "Well, I'm afraid that's light out for Dadster." He delivers a series of instructions about where I am to find the stowed blankets, and reiterates the importance of turning out the lamp before I fall asleep. He crawls into his sleeping berth, which is like a little cave at the pointed bow of the boat. I can see only the bottoms of his feet.

I am left effectively alone in the little cabin. I know the waves outside are rough only because my drink is sloshing in my glass—a little amber sea with a maraschino shipwreck rocking at the bottom. My landsick inner ears report that *The Mary M* is steady as a sober hand.

I imagine that my cresting revelation is a tired one for film students, maybe sociology majors too.

I don't know who the film star was—though Rudolph Valentino seems a likely candidate. Heartthrob. Italian. Died young and suddenly, inciting a wave of hysterical grief. But I'm not a film buff. Really, I can't even confirm the veracity of the story. The problems multiplying in my head, however, don't depend on the story being true.

This is certain: only the most recent generations have been confronted with images—still and moving— of their dead. These images invest the dead with just as much vivacity as we possess ourselves. There is Valentino lighting his cigarette, tapping it twice against the case. There he is bare-chested, in a rage. And there is smirking Valentino preparing to seduce the dancing girl—all the while completely unaware that he is dead.

It's hard to muster the imagination to really endow feudal serfs with all the nuance and passion of the living. They're just too far gone, and the implements they left behind do nothing to conjure a compelling impression their humanity. Ox-drawn plows do not arouse us. But through movies and pictures, you can laugh with dead people, or tear up, or get hard. The sexual aspect—that's important. Voltaire exists in my imagination as a wry and amusing brain in a vat, a would-be sparring companion. But there's no virility to him. And entities that are purely intellectual, well they might not be terribly affected by dying—they're rather incorporeal to start with. But people with muscular forearms, people with tans, people who can arch one eyebrow in perfect isolation, people with really good comic timing, these are individuals with appetite. These are real people, like me and my friends.

It's harder to feel important in the presence of so many people, dead and alive. Trading images across oceans, and even from the grave, increases our perceived size of the human community. I am real; my mom is real; now this kid on Youtube is real. This film star from Bollywood who is apparently the most famous person on earth—although I have never heard of her—she is real. Rudolph and the dancing girl, I cannot deny them as I have denied the serfs. We are each a lonely numerator in a fraction whose denominator is always increasing—spinning ever upward like one of those tickers that calculate debt.

The prospect of having a very small role in the world is at odds with our intuitions about our own importance. Even the design of our bodies reinforces the idea that we are crucial players. By the literal report of our senses, nothing actually happens without us. You have no experience when you're not around. The world is quiet when you sleep. It parts around you as you maneuver through it, leaving your intelligence to presume that it zips itself together after you have passed. Our vision, the perceived seat of consciousness, seems to powerfully manipulate the world. Objects of interest obligingly grow larger as we approach, lending themselves to our inspection. When we are through, they collapse to into the distance, to be stowed beneath the horizon.

Then a cameraman arrives. He unveils an unending catalog of realistic pictures from other lives and it becomes increasingly difficult to believe that we occupy a central position. Daguerre, when he took the first portrait of a Parisian passing by, became the Copernicus of the personal sphere.

And now there are so many pictures of so many real people, that I cannot possibly consider all of them. Even walking down a crowded street, I don't have the mental or emotive capacity to invest everybody with the same sensitivity, nuance, and depth that I experience. I just don't think we have the RAM. In his book *The Conquest of Happiness*, Bertrand Russell wrote: "The natural instinct of man, as of other animals, is to investigate every stranger of his species with a view to deciding whether to behave to him in a friendly or hostile manner. This instinct has to be inhibited by those who travel in the subway." He goes on to say that the suppression of all this instinct is really very draining—a primary source of fatigue in the modern world. Before cities and civilizations, I don't know how many strangers a human being would be likely to encounter in the wild. It seems safe to guess that if I asked an anthropologist her answer would be way less than "A million." We're maxed out by all the new faces: on the subway, on the magazines, on our homepage. We just have to treat these people as stand-ins for real people until we have the opportunity to become personally acquainted. We do the same kind of thinking when we deal with complicated concepts of physics or math. We can say 'infinity,' but really the word is just a placeholder for an ignorance whose parameters we have taped off in our heads. We can't firmly grasp 'eternity' or 'humanity,' so we assign a word to the empty cage in our imaginations and continue down the aisle.

In this way, our understanding of the human world balloons and then collapses. At some point in our development we come to appreciate that there are more real people than we can name or imagine. We realize that ours are probably not speaking roles. And so we venture off to stage a little side project with the other extras.

We reduce the scope of our interest and consideration to the living, and to the people who seem to have some reciprocal interest in us. We bear witness to one another's lives, to the attendant losses and enthusiasms. We endure dragging dance recitals; attend parent-teacher conferences; and photograph the graduation march. And when we're old enough to return the favor, we drive north to spend some days aboard a nauseating sailboat, and we watch ourselves go grey in the shadow of an unseen hand.

Thank You.

To my readers: Jaclyn Khoury, Brian Bieber, Kai Benson, Maxwell Wander, and Bradley Kenneth Baron.

To John Samels, of Desk2, for the design. www.desk-2.com.

To my parents for allowing me to sit with you and your friends—the kids table is miserable.

To Ben Cohen for the moving pictures.

To *The Vestal Review*, which first published "Alice Drowning."

To Jon Hester for the big help on short notice.

To the Minnesota State Arts Board for the support.

To Doomtree for the ethic and the privilege.

About the Author

Dessa is a member of the Doomtree crew, an instructor at the McNally Smith College of Music, and is pretty sure she's a secular humanist.

If you enjoyed *Spiral Bound,* you might also like:

· *This American Life* hosted by Ira Glass
· *Willful Creatures* by Aimee Bender
· *For the Time Being* by Annie Dillard
· Everything by Malcolm Gladwell
· Amaretto with whiskey, on ice

To stay abreast of Dessa's music and writing, visit www.doomtree.net or myspace.com/dessa.